HOW TO RAIS

Flock Dynamics: Understanding Social Behavior and Herd Management

Michael K. Jumper

Copyright © 2024 by Michael K. Jumper

All rights reserved

No part of this publication may be reproduced, stored in a retrieval system. or transmitted. in and form or by any means, electronic, mechanical, photocopying, or otherwise, without the prior written permission of the author.

The information in this ebook is true and complete to the best of our knowledge. All recommendations are made without guarantee on the part of the author or publisher. The author and publisher disclaim any liability in connection with the use of this information

TABLE OF CONTENTS

Introduction 7

Chapter 1 10

    Getting Started 10

        Introduction to sheep Farming 10

        Benefits of Sheep farming 12

            Economic Viability 12

            Environmental Sustainability 12

            Versatility of Products 13

            Adaptability to Diverse Climates and Settings 13

            Small Land Requirements 13

            Community and Lifestyle Benefits 14

        Understanding Sheep Behavior and Traits 15

        The Economics of Sheep Farming: Cost and Revenue Analysis 18

Chapter 2 20

    Choosing Your Sheep 20

        Types of Sheep Breeds and Their Purposes 20

            Merino Sheep 20

            Suffolk Sheep 20

            Dorset Sheep 20

Hampshire Sheep 21

East Friesian Sheep 21

Katahdin Sheep 21

Shetland Sheep 22

Romney Sheep 22

Factors to Consider When Selecting Sheep 23

Where to Purchase Healthy Sheep 26

Chapter 3 28

Basic Sheep Care 28

Daily Care Requirements 28

Nutritional Needs: Feed and Water 30

Shelter and Space Requirements 32

Chapter 4 34

Health Management 34

Common Sheep Diseases and Prevention 34

Vaccinations and Routine Health Checks 36

Dealing with Parasites and Other Common Health Issues. 38

Chapter 5 40

Reproduction and Breeding 40

Understanding the Breeding Cycle 40

Techniques for Effective Breeding 43

Caring for Ewes During Pregnancy 46

Managing Lambing Season 49

Chapter 6 52

Flock Management 52

Herd Dynamics and Behavior Management 52

Training and Handling Techniques 55

Tools and Equipment Needed for Effective Flock Management 57

Chapter 7 59

Wool and Shearing 59

Best Practices for Wool Production 59

Shearing Techniques and Tools 62

Processing and Selling Wool 65

Chapter 8 68

Marketing Your Products 68

Understanding the Market for Sheep Products 68

Strategies for Marketing Meat, Wool, and Live Animals ... 71

Online and Offline Marketing Techniques 74

Chapter 9 77

Pasture and Land Management 77

Basics of Pasture Layout and Design 77

Rotational Grazing Systems 79

Land Maintenance and Sustainability Practices 82

Chapter 10 85

Legal and Financial Management 85

Understanding Local Regulations and Permits 85

Financial Planning and Record Keeping 88

Risk Management and Insurance for Sheep Farms 91

Chapter 11 94

Conclusion 94

INTRODUCTION

In the verdant valleys of Green Meadows, Sam Connors embarked on a new journey. After years as a city accountant, he decided to shift gears and pursue his dream of living off the land. He bought a quaint farm and ten sheep, inspired by visions of sustainable living and peaceful countryside retreats. However, Sam soon realized that sheep farming was more complex and challenging than he had imagined.

From unexpected illnesses that plagued his flock to the chaos of the lambing season, Sam felt overwhelmed and underprepared. He needed guidance, and he found it in a pivotal book titled "How to Raise Sheep."

This wasn't just any farming manual; it was a comprehensive guide that felt like a wise friend walking beside him through each step of his sheep farming journey. The book started with an engaging introduction that not only captured the joy and benefits of sheep farming but also outlined the rich, fulfilling life that awaited those who embraced the shepherd's path.

As Sam flipped through the pages, he discovered invaluable advice that transformed his farming experience. He learned about the unique behaviors and needs of his sheep, allowing him to cater to their specific requirements and personalities. The book also provided crucial insights into the nutritional needs of sheep, helping Sam to devise a diet plan that boosted the health and vitality of his flock.

The lambing season, which had initially seemed daunting, became manageable with the book's detailed explanations and practical tips. Sam learned to recognize the signs of labor, provide necessary care during and after birth, and ensure the health of both ewes and lambs. This guidance not only saved lives but also enriched Sam's experience as a farmer.

Shearing, which Sam had once viewed as a cumbersome chore, turned into a rewarding aspect of his business. The book taught him efficient shearing techniques and offered strategies for processing and marketing the wool, turning a routine task into a profitable venture.

"How to Raise Sheep" covered every aspect of sheep farming, from day-to-day care to the broader strokes of farm management and marketing. It equipped Sam with the knowledge to not only care for his flock but also to navigate the business side of farming effectively.

Why should someone buy this book? For anyone standing at the threshold of sheep farming, whether a novice with a dream or a farmer seeking to expand, this book offers not just knowledge but a transformation into a capable and confident shepherd. It's more than a manual; it's a mentor.

For Sam, the book was not just a purchase; it was an investment in a new lifestyle—one that brought him closer to nature, gave him peace, and provided a sustainable living. This book isn't just about raising sheep; it's about cultivating a life of fulfillment, peace, and prosperity. Whether you're looking to start a small hobby farm or a large commercial operation, "How to Raise Sheep" is your comprehensive guide to mastering the art of sheep farming.

CHAPTER 1

Getting Started

Introduction to sheep Farming

Sheep farming presents a unique opportunity for individuals interested in agriculture to dive into a sector that is not only profitable but also enriching to the lifestyle of those who embrace it. Getting started in sheep farming requires a basic understanding of sheep behavior, the financial implications of setting up and maintaining a sheep farm, and the various benefits that come with it.

Sheep are known for their docile temperament, making them ideal for novice farmers. They are also relatively low maintenance compared to other livestock, consuming a wide variety of forage and being adaptable to various climatic conditions. This adaptability makes sheep farming viable across a diverse range of geographical locations. Farmers can raise sheep for various products including wool, meat, and milk, which broadens the market opportunities.

Financially, starting a sheep farm can be less daunting than other agricultural ventures. Initial investments include purchasing land if not already owned, building or adapting existing structures for sheep housing, acquiring the sheep, and setting up feeding and health management systems. The ongoing costs include feed, veterinary care, and labor, but these are generally manageable. Sheep farming also benefits from several government grants and subsidies, which can ease the financial burden on new farmers.

The economic benefits of sheep farming extend beyond simple profitability. Sheep products like wool and lamb meat have a consistent demand in markets around the world. Wool, especially, is a renewable resource that can be harvested annually without harming the sheep, making it a sustainable choice for environmentally conscious farmers. Moreover, sheep manure is an excellent fertilizer, enhancing soil fertility without the need for chemical fertilizers.

Sheep farming also contributes positively to the environment. Sheep grazing can help manage land and control bush encroachment, which in turn supports biodiversity. Properly managed sheep farms can lead to enhanced land health, reducing erosion and increasing the organic content of the soil.

Benefits of Sheep farming

Sheep farming offers numerous benefits that appeal to a wide range of individuals—from those looking to supplement their income to others seeking a more sustainable lifestyle. Here is a closer look at some of the major advantages.

Economic Viability

Sheep are relatively low-cost animals to purchase and maintain, making them an excellent option for aspiring farmers on a budget. Their upkeep requires less feed compared to larger livestock like cattle, and they can often graze on pasture that is unsuitable for other uses. The economic return from sheep comes not only from selling meat and wool but also from milk products and breeding stock, which can be highly profitable markets.

Environmental Sustainability

Sheep farming can be an environmentally sustainable practice. Sheep naturally graze and can help control weed growth, reducing the need for chemical herbicides. Their grazing can also aid in maintaining healthy soil by naturally fertilizing the land and promoting the growth of native plants. This helps improve the overall biodiversity of the farming area, enhancing soil structure and fertility without the intensive use of artificial inputs.

Versatility of Products

Sheep produce a variety of products that are in demand. Wool is perhaps the best-known product, renowned for its insulation properties and used in everything from clothing to blankets. Sheep meat, or lamb and mutton, is a staple in many diets around the world and is celebrated for its distinct flavor. Additionally, sheep's milk is highly nutritious and can be used to make cheeses like Roquefort and feta, which are prized in both domestic and international markets.

Adaptability to Diverse Climates and Settings

Sheep are remarkably adaptable creatures, capable of thriving in a variety of climates and environments. From the cold reaches of Scotland to the arid regions of Australia, sheep have shown that they can adapt and thrive. This adaptability makes them a viable agricultural option for many areas of the United States, ranging from the cool, wet climates of the Northwest to the hotter, drier regions of the Southwest.

Small Land Requirements

Unlike larger livestock, sheep do not require vast amounts of land. They can be raised successfully on small plots of pasture, making them ideal for small-scale farmers or those with limited land resources. This smaller land requirement also makes sheep farming an accessible venture for new farmers who might not have the capital to invest in larger, more land-intensive types of farming.

Community and Lifestyle Benefits

Sheep farming can contribute to a lifestyle that many find deeply rewarding. It allows individuals and families to work closely with animals and nature, which can be both therapeutic and fulfilling. The rhythm of seasonal farming tasks, such as lambing and shearing, provides a connection to the natural world that is often lost in urban settings. Furthermore, sheep farming can help strengthen local economies by providing jobs and supporting local agricultural businesses.

Understanding Sheep Behavior and Traits

Sheep are social animals with behavior patterns deeply rooted in flock mentality, which is essential for their protection and survival. Unlike the solitary instincts seen in other species, sheep rely heavily on group cohesion to feel secure and stress-free. Recognizing the fundamental behaviors and traits of sheep is crucial for any farmer, as it not only impacts their welfare but also the productivity and ease of managing a flock.

Firstly, understanding the hierarchical structure within a flock can greatly enhance management strategies. Sheep establish a social pecking order that influences their grazing, breeding, and general interaction patterns. Observing your sheep can help identify leaders and more submissive animals, allowing for better management of feeding and mating practices. Dominant sheep often eat first and choose the best grazing areas, while subordinate ones wait their turn. This behavior can affect the nutritional intake of less dominant animals, making strategic feeding practices necessary to ensure all sheep receive adequate nutrition.

Sheep are also creatures of habit and prefer a structured routine, which can be leveraged to reduce stress during activities like feeding, milking, or moving them between pastures. Changes in their environment or daily routine can lead to stress, which manifests in physical symptoms such as weight loss or decreased fertility. Therefore, keeping a consistent routine helps maintain a calm and productive flock.

The flight zone of sheep, or their personal space, is another critical aspect of their behavior. This invisible boundary varies from one sheep to another and understanding it is vital for handling. When a person enters this zone, the sheep's natural response is to flee. The size of the flight zone can indicate the animal's level of tameness; a large flight zone suggests a wilder, less accustomed sheep to human presence, while a smaller one indicates familiarity and comfort with human interaction. Properly managing this can make routine handling and medical treatments much more manageable.

Communication among sheep, primarily through vocalizations and body language, plays a significant role in their social structure. They make different sounds to alert others about potential threats, call their lambs, or express discomfort. Recognizing these sounds can help in early identification of issues such as predators or health problems.

Breeding behavior is another area where knowledge of sheep traits is invaluable. Ewes exhibit specific signs when in heat, such as increased vocalization or restlessness, and understanding these signs can maximize breeding success. Rams, on the other hand, show interest in ewes in heat through sniffing and following them more closely. Managing this behavior by keeping rams and ewes separate until the optimal time for breeding ensures effective and controlled reproduction.

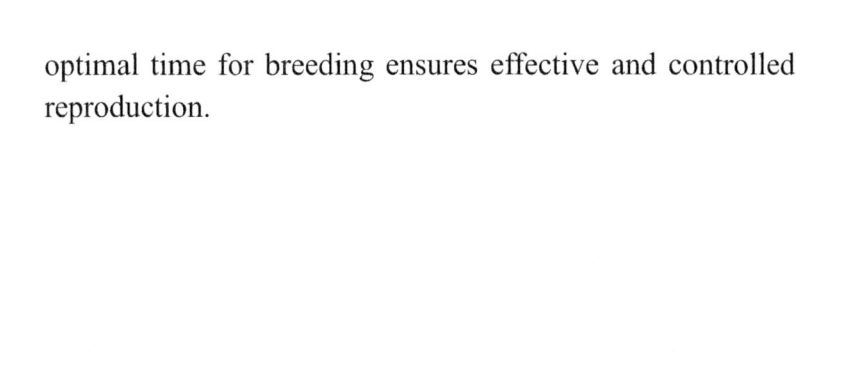

The Economics of Sheep Farming: Cost and Revenue Analysis

Sheep farming can be a profitable venture, but like any agricultural business, it requires a thorough understanding of both initial investments and ongoing costs versus potential revenues. When starting a sheep farm, one of the first expenses to consider is the cost of the land. Depending on the region, land suitable for grazing can vary widely in price. Additionally, the size of the land directly impacts the number of sheep it can sustain, which in turn affects potential income.

After securing land, the next significant investment is the sheep themselves. The price of sheep varies based on breed, age, health, and market demand. Purebred and registered sheep typically cost more but can also yield higher returns through breeding programs and premium wool. Start-up costs also include fencing, shelter, and initial feed and veterinary care. Fencing must be sturdy and safe to prevent escapes and protect the flock from predators, while shelter needs to be adequate to shield the sheep from harsh weather.

Ongoing costs include feed, which can fluctuate based on market prices and seasonal availability. While sheep primarily graze, supplementary feed may be necessary during the winter or in areas with poor pasture quality. Regular veterinary care is crucial to maintain the health of the flock and includes vaccinations, parasite control, and emergency health services.

On the revenue side, sheep farming income can come from several sources. The primary one is meat production, with lamb typically commanding a higher market price than mutton. Wool is another significant source of income, especially for breeds known for high-quality fleece. Specialty wools can fetch premium prices. In addition to meat and wool, breeding stock can also be sold, particularly if the farmer has high-quality, genetically superior animals that are in demand.

Diversifying income sources can help stabilize the farm's finances. For example, offering agritourism activities, such as farm tours or shearing demonstrations, can provide additional revenue streams. Agri-tourism not only helps in marketing the farm's primary products but also spreads risk.

Profitability in sheep farming also depends on efficient herd management, minimizing mortality rates, and optimizing reproductive performance. Good management practices, including rotational grazing to maintain pasture health, can reduce feed costs and improve the overall productivity of the farm.

CHAPTER 2

Choosing Your Sheep

Types of Sheep Breeds and Their Purposes

Merino Sheep

Merino sheep are prized for their wool, which is among the finest and softest of any sheep. The fibers are exceptionally fine, making them ideal for creating high-quality, luxurious textiles. Merinos are also quite hardy and adaptable, capable of thriving in both cold and hot climates. They have a high fleece yield, often requiring shearing at least once a year due to the rapid growth of their wool. In terms of temperament, Merinos are generally docile, making them easy to manage.

Suffolk Sheep

Suffolk sheep are primarily known for their meat production. They exhibit a rapid growth rate, making them a popular choice for meat farmers looking for efficient turnaround. Suffolks have a distinctive appearance with their unwooled, black faces and legs, which contrast sharply with their white bodies. They are robust and muscular, with a high yield of lean meat, and their docile nature contributes to easy handling and management on farms.

Dorset Sheep

Dorsets are extremely versatile, capable of producing both meat and wool. They have a medium wool type that is dense and good quality, though not as fine as that of the

Merino. A unique characteristic of Dorset sheep is their ability to breed year-round (polled Dorsets), which allows for more flexible management of reproduction and lambing. They are known for their good mothering capabilities and generally calm disposition.

Hampshire Sheep

Hampshires are another meat breed, recognized for their large, muscular build. They have a dark face and ears, with a wool cap that is quite distinctive. The wool of Hampshire sheep is coarser and used primarily in wool blends. They are known for their vigorous growth rate and excellent feed efficiency, making them popular in commercial meat production settings.

East Friesian Sheep

East Friesians are the gold standard for dairy sheep, producing more milk than any other breed. Their milk has a high butterfat content, which is excellent for making rich cheeses and yogurts. These sheep are larger and more docile than most dairy breeds, with a calm temperament that makes them easy to milk. They have a higher lambing rate, often producing twins or triplets, which enhances their productivity in a dairy setting.

Katahdin Sheep

Katahdins are a hair breed, which means they do not grow wool and do not require shearing. They are particularly valued for their low-maintenance characteristics, making them ideal for farms focused on easy care and pasture management. Katahdins are resistant to many common sheep diseases and are known for their adaptability to various climates and conditions. They are primarily used for meat, which is lean and mild in flavor.

Shetland Sheep

Shetland sheep are small and resilient, known for surviving harsh conditions in the Shetland Islands. They produce a fine, soft wool that comes in a variety of natural colors, highly valued by hand spinners and knitters. Shetlands are also used for meat, though they are smaller in size. Their ability to thrive on sparse grazing makes them excellent for land management in less fertile areas.

Romney Sheep

Romney sheep are well-suited to wet, marshy conditions where other breeds might struggle. They have a long, lustrous fleece that is highly resistant to moisture, making their wool ideal for spinning and felting. Romney wool is known for its strength, which makes it suitable for a variety of textile products. Romneys are also good meat producers, with a calm nature that makes them easy to handle.

Factors to Consider When Selecting Sheep

Selecting the right sheep for your farm involves a careful evaluation of various factors that directly impact the success and sustainability of your flock. Understanding and prioritizing these factors ensure that you invest in animals that will thrive in your specific environment and meet your farming objectives. Let's delve deeper into each of these critical considerations.

Breed Choice directly correlates with your farming goals. Different sheep breeds excel in specific areas; for example, the Rambouillet is known for its superior wool quality, making it ideal for wool-focused farming. On the other hand, breeds like Texel or Dorset are prized for their meat quality. If dairy production is your goal, consider breeds like the East Friesian. Additionally, some breeds like the Shetland are dual-purpose, good for both wool and meat, offering versatility. Understanding the strengths and typical uses of each breed can guide your selection process to align with your production needs.

Climate Adaptability is crucial since sheep must be comfortable in their environment to maximize productivity. Breeds have evolved characteristics suited to specific climates—a critical consideration as these traits affect survival and productivity. For instance, sheep with thicker, denser wool coats are better suited for cold climates but may suffer in heat unless managed carefully. Conversely, hair sheep, like the Katahdin, which have hair instead of wool, are better suited for hot climates due to their increased heat tolerance.

Breeding Stock Quality affects the genetic makeup and future productivity of your flock. When selecting breeding stock, it's essential to evaluate the genetic lineage for traits such as robust health, high fertility, and quality of meat or wool. Look for breeders who practice selective breeding to enhance these desirable traits and can provide detailed records of ancestry and health status, which can indicate potential longevity and productivity of the sheep.

Fertility and Reproduction are fundamental for flock expansion and sustainability. Evaluate the historical fertility rates and lambing records of potential stock. Some breeds are known for higher twinning rates, which can significantly increase flock size and profitability. Understanding the reproductive traits of your breed helps in planning for breeding and lambing infrastructure.

Temperament plays a significant role in flock management. Sheep temperament can vary widely from one breed to another and even among individuals within a breed. Easier handling and management come with more docile sheep, reducing stress for both the animals and the handlers. Sheep with calm demeanors are particularly important in settings where frequent human interaction is necessary.

Health Resilience is a factor that can significantly influence maintenance costs and flock longevity. Choose breeds known for their resistance to diseases and parasites prevalent in your area. This consideration will help reduce veterinary costs and minimize flock mortality rates. Check for breeds that have adapted to local conditions over generations, as these animals are more likely to possess natural resistances to local health challenges.

Physical Attributes such as size, body condition, and structural soundness are indicators of good health and should be carefully inspected. Animals should display a robust physique with well-maintained wool or hair, clear eyes, and good dentition, which suggest overall health and vitality. The physical condition can also affect the animal's ability to graze and reproduce effectively.

Local Availability of breeds affects initial investment costs and ease of purchase. Opting for breeds that are readily available in your area not only supports local breeders but also ensures that the sheep are pre-adapted to the local environment. This can lead to better survival rates and reduced adaptation stress for the animals.

Where to Purchase Healthy Sheep

When you're ready to begin your sheep farming journey, purchasing healthy sheep is crucial. Healthy sheep are not only more productive, but they also require less intervention and cost in terms of healthcare, making your farming venture more sustainable and enjoyable. Here are some tips on how to find and select healthy sheep.

Begin your search by exploring local farms. Purchasing sheep from local breeders not only supports the local economy, but also reduces the stress on animals that often accompanies long transportation. Local breeders with a good reputation are likely to offer healthier sheep that are adapted to your area's climate and conditions. You can find these breeders through agricultural extension services, livestock associations, or local farming groups.

Attending sheep and livestock auctions can be another source for purchasing sheep, but it requires a keen eye to ensure the health of the animals. It's advisable to visit several auctions to observe the animals and talk to the sellers before making a purchase. Look for animals that are active, alert, and have a healthy coat. Avoid sheep that appear lethargic, have patchy coats, or show signs of physical abnormalities.

Another option is to connect with sheep farmers online. Many breeders maintain active online presences where they list available animals along with detailed health records and breeding history. Websites like Livestock Conservancy or local farm networks can also be useful. However, when buying sheep online, it's important to ensure that you can either visit the farm or see comprehensive visual documentation of the sheep's health and living conditions before finalizing the purchase.

When selecting sheep, pay special attention to the animal's health records, which should be transparent and complete. Ask the breeder about any past illnesses, the vaccinations that the sheep have received, and the general healthcare routine the flock follows. A trustworthy breeder will be open about their herd's health status and the preventive measures they employ.

Moreover, inspect the sheep for signs of good health. Healthy sheep should have bright eyes, clean noses, and an even, full coat of wool or hair, depending on the breed. Their movement should be energetic and coordinated. Check the condition of their hooves, which should be well-trimmed and free of cracks. Listen for any signs of coughing or labored breathing, which could indicate respiratory issues.

Finally, consider the sheep's temperament, as it can significantly affect handling and management. Sheep that are calm and easy to handle can make daily farm operations much smoother. Spend time observing the sheep's behavior in their environment and interacting with them if possible.

CHAPTER 3

Basic Sheep Care

Daily Care Requirements

Sheep require attentive daily care to ensure their health and well-being, which is critical for a successful farming operation. One of the primary daily tasks involves providing fresh water and appropriate nutrition. Sheep typically graze on pasture, but their dietary needs can vary based on age, health, and whether they are pregnant or lactating. It's essential to offer a balanced diet that may include pasture grass, supplemented with hay, especially during the winter or dry seasons when fresh grass isn't available. Additionally, providing a mineral supplement can help prevent deficiencies that might otherwise lead to health issues.

Feeding routines should be consistent, with feeds given at the same times each day to help maintain the digestive health of the sheep. This regularity also helps in monitoring their health, as changes in appetite can be early indicators of illness. Besides their diet, it's important to check water sources daily to ensure they are clean and unfrozen.

Beyond feeding, daily inspections are crucial for maintaining sheep health. This involves observing each sheep for signs of illness or distress such as limping, abnormal behavior, or changes in eating habits. Early detection of health issues, such as foot rot or flystrike, significantly increases the effectiveness of treatment and reduces the potential for serious complications.

Proper shelter is another vital aspect of daily care. Sheep need protection from severe weather conditions, whether it's excessive heat or cold, rain, or snow. Their shelter should be dry and well-ventilated, free from drafts, dampness, and ammonia buildup, which can cause respiratory issues. Regular cleaning of the shelter is necessary to prevent the buildup of manure and to control parasites and other infectious agents.

Parasite management is an ongoing concern in sheep care. Farmers must conduct regular checks for signs of parasite infestation, such as anemia or bottle jaw, and implement a deworming schedule based on veterinary advice. It's also important to rotate pastures to help reduce the load of parasites in the environment, which can prevent many health issues related to parasitic infections.

Lastly, shepherds should always be gentle and calm around their sheep to keep them from stressing, as stress can lead to a host of health problems and poor productivity. Handling sheep regularly but calmly helps in managing them more effectively, especially during shearing, medical treatments, or when moving them between pastures.

Nutritional Needs: Feed and Water

Sheep are versatile animals that adapt well to a variety of climates and conditions, but their health and productivity depend heavily on proper nutrition. The foundation of good sheep nutrition includes balanced feed and adequate water supply. Understanding the dietary requirements of sheep and ensuring they have access to these essentials can significantly influence their health, growth, and the quality of the wool and meat they produce.

Sheep primarily consume a diet rich in fibers and are natural grazers, which means they do best on a pasture-based diet. Pasture grasses and other forages such as hay are typical components of a sheep's diet and provide the necessary nutrients and minerals. During the grazing season, sheep can obtain almost all their nutritional needs from pasture alone, provided that the pasture is well-managed and the grass quality is high. In winter or during droughts when natural forages are not available, supplemental feeding with hay or haylage is essential to maintain the health of the flock.

The nutritional needs of sheep vary depending on their age, breed, health status, and whether they are pregnant or lactating. Lambs require a diet rich in protein to support rapid growth and development, while mature sheep need a maintenance diet that keeps them healthy but prevents excessive weight gain, which could lead to health issues. Ewes require additional nutrients during pregnancy and lactation to support the development of lambs and the production of milk.

Grains such as corn, oats, and barley are often used as supplemental feed for sheep to provide extra energy, particularly for breeding rams during mating season or for pregnant ewes in the last trimester of gestation. However, it's important to introduce grains gradually into their diet to prevent digestive upset, as sheep's stomachs are sensitive to sudden changes in feed.

Minerals and vitamins are critical components of a sheep's diet. Sheep require a variety of trace minerals including selenium, zinc, copper, and iodine. However, copper is toxic to sheep in large quantities, and care should be taken with mineral supplements to ensure they are formulated specifically for sheep. Vitamin supplementation, particularly vitamins A, D, and E, may be necessary, especially in regions with long winters where natural sunlight, which helps animals synthesize vitamin D, is scarce.

Water is as crucial as food for sheep. They need a constant supply of clean, fresh water to stay hydrated and maintain bodily functions. Water consumption varies depending on the weather, with sheep drinking more in hot conditions and less in cold weather. Lactating ewes have the highest water requirements due to the demands of milk production.

Shelter and Space Requirements

Sheep are relatively low-maintenance livestock, but providing them with the right shelter and space is crucial for their health and productivity. Sheep need protection from extreme weather conditions such as rain, snow, heat, and cold, which can affect their well-being and growth. A well-designed shelter also protects sheep from predators and provides a safe, comfortable environment for lambing and routine care.

The basic requirement for sheep housing is that it must keep the sheep dry and provide adequate ventilation. Moisture is a significant enemy of sheep, as it can lead to health issues like hoof rot and respiratory illnesses. The shelter should have a roof that prevents rain from entering and walls that block prevailing winds, especially in colder climates. The flooring should be elevated and designed to drain well; it should also be easy to clean and maintain.

Ventilation is another critical factor. Poor ventilation can cause a buildup of dampness and ammonia from urine and manure, which can harm the respiratory health of the sheep. The shelter should allow for natural air circulation without causing drafts, particularly where young lambs are present.

Space requirements vary depending on the breed and size of the sheep, the type of production (meat, milk, or wool), and whether the sheep are grazed extensively or intensively managed. Generally, each sheep requires between 15 to 20 square feet of covered shelter. This space should be increased to about 25 square feet per ewe with lambs to provide adequate room for nursing and growth without causing stress or competition for space.

For outdoor space, it's ideal to have at least one acre of pasture for every five to ten sheep, allowing for rotational grazing. Rotational grazing helps manage pasture wear and tear, prevents overgrazing, and reduces the risk of parasite load, which can be a significant health issue in densely stocked areas. Pastures should be fenced adequately to keep sheep in and predators out. Fencing should be sheep-proof, sturdy, and regularly inspected for damage.

Water access is a part of space planning. Sheep need a constant supply of clean, fresh water, which can be provided via automatic watering systems or troughs that are cleaned and refilled regularly. The water sources should be easily accessible to all sheep, including lambs.

Sheep are social animals and thrive in a flock environment, so their space should be designed to accommodate group dynamics and behaviors. Providing enough room for all sheep to rest, feed, and socialize without excessive competition is vital for maintaining a healthy and productive flock.

CHAPTER 4

Health Management

Common Sheep Diseases and Prevention

Sheep are susceptible to a variety of diseases, each requiring specific management strategies for prevention and control. Among the most common ailments are foot rot, scrapie, bluetongue, and pneumonia, each posing significant threats to the health and productivity of a flock.

Foot rot is a highly infectious bacterial condition that causes lameness in affected sheep. It is caused by the interaction of two bacteria, Dichelobacter nodosus and Fusobacterium necrophorum, which thrive in wet, dirty ground conditions. The disease results in severe pain and can lead to weight loss and reduced wool quality due to the animal's decreased ability to graze. Prevention focuses on maintaining dry, well-drained pasture environments and regular hoof trimming and inspections to catch and treat infections early. Footbaths containing zinc sulfate can be used as a preventive measure during wet seasons.

Scrapie is a fatal, degenerative disease affecting the central nervous system of sheep and is part of a group of diseases known as transmissible spongiform encephalopathies (TSEs). It is unique among the TSEs because it can be transmitted through infected sheep's placenta and bodily fluids. Symptoms include intense itching, wool pulling, aggression, lip smacking, and eventual inability to stand. There is no cure for scrapie, and infected animals must be culled to prevent spread. Breeding programs now often focus on selecting for genetic resistance to scrapie, and strict regulations govern the handling and disposal of scrapie-affected animals.

Bluetongue is caused by a virus transmitted by biting midges, which breed near stagnant water. The disease is not contagious from sheep to sheep but spreads through insect vectors. Symptoms include high fever, excessive salivation, swollen lips and tongue, and lameness. While bluetongue can be fatal, vaccines are available and effective in preventing the disease. Vector control through the management of water sources and the use of insect repellents during outbreak periods is also crucial.

Pneumonia in sheep can be caused by a variety of bacterial, viral, and environmental factors, often exacerbated by poor ventilation in housing, stressful transportation, or sudden changes in the weather. Symptoms include coughing, difficulty breathing, nasal discharge, and lethargy. Treatment involves antibiotics and supportive care, but prevention is best achieved by ensuring good ventilation in living quarters, minimizing stress for the animals, and keeping good overall flock health to prevent opportunistic infections.

Vaccinations and Routine Health Checks

Vaccinations are crucial in sheep farming as they help prevent a range of common and potentially fatal diseases. For new sheep farmers, understanding which vaccines to administer and when to do so is essential for maintaining a healthy flock. Typically, sheep are vaccinated against clostridial diseases, which include tetanus and pulpy kidney disease. These vaccinations often begin early in the lamb's life, usually within the first few weeks, with booster shots given at intervals specified by the vaccine manufacturer.

Another important vaccine for sheep is against footrot, a painful condition caused by bacteria that can severely affect hoof health and mobility. This vaccine is particularly crucial in wet climates where the disease is more prevalent. Depending on the presence of other specific health risks in the area, such as bluetongue virus or pneumonia, additional vaccinations might be necessary. It is best to consult with a local veterinarian to determine the precise vaccinations needed based on regional disease risks and the specific conditions of the farm.

Routine health checks are equally important in managing a healthy sheep flock. These checks allow for the early detection and treatment of issues before they become severe. Regular health assessments should include checking the condition of the sheep's teeth, hooves, and wool, as well as monitoring for signs of infections or parasites. Weight checks are also a critical part of these examinations to ensure that each sheep is maintaining a healthy weight, which is a good indicator of overall health.

Parasite control is another key aspect of sheep health management. Sheep can be susceptible to both internal and external parasites, including worms, lice, and flies. Fecal tests are a common method for monitoring worm burdens in the flock, and should be conducted several times a year to help manage deworming treatments effectively. Strategic use of antiparasitic medications, often in conjunction with pasture management techniques such as rotational grazing, can help reduce the incidence of parasitic infections.

Furthermore, maintaining detailed health records for each animal is crucial. These records should include information on vaccination dates, any medical treatments, results of health checks, and notes on individual animal health incidents. Good record-keeping can aid in the early identification of patterns that might indicate broader health issues within the flock.

Dealing with Parasites and Other Common Health Issues

Sheep are susceptible to a variety of parasites and common health issues that can affect their well-being and productivity. Among the most prevalent challenges are gastrointestinal worms, external parasites like ticks and lice, and other health issues such as foot rot and pneumonia. Understanding how to manage these effectively is crucial for maintaining a healthy flock.

Gastrointestinal parasites, particularly worms, are a major concern in sheep farming. These parasites can cause malnutrition, weight loss, and in severe cases, death. Regular deworming is essential and should be based on the specific needs of the flock and the local environment. Fecal egg count tests are a valuable tool for determining the burden of parasites and the effectiveness of the deworming protocol. Rotating pastures and avoiding overgrazing also help reduce the risk of infection, as parasites often proliferate in heavily grazed areas where sheep are in close contact with contaminated soil.

External parasites such as ticks, lice, and mites can cause irritation, skin infections, and in severe cases, anemia. Managing these involves regular inspections of the flock and treating with appropriate insecticides. It's important to follow the manufacturer's guidelines closely to ensure effectiveness and safety. Additionally, maintaining clean bedding and stable environments helps minimize the risk of infestation.

Foot rot is another common issue, caused by bacteria that thrive in wet, dirty conditions. This painful condition can lead to lameness and reduced mobility. To prevent foot rot, farmers should ensure that their sheep have access to dry, well-drained standing areas, especially during wet weather. Regular hoof trimming and foot baths with antibacterial solutions can also prevent the onset of foot rot.

Respiratory issues such as pneumonia are particularly dangerous in sheep, often exacerbated by poor ventilation in housing, stress, and sudden changes in weather. Ensuring adequate airflow in barns and shelters and providing a stress-free environment with ample space can help reduce the incidence of respiratory problems. Vaccinations may also be advisable, depending on local conditions and the specific risks faced by the flock.

In addition to these specific issues, a general health check regime is vital. This includes regular body condition scoring to monitor the nutritional status of each sheep, along with vaccinations and other preventive care measures. Keeping detailed health records helps in monitoring the health status over time and can be invaluable in diagnosing and treating problems early.

CHAPTER 5

Reproduction and Breeding

Understanding the Breeding Cycle

Understanding the breeding cycle of sheep is crucial for effective flock management and ensuring the health and productivity of both ewes and rams. Sheep have a seasonal breeding pattern, typically entering their breeding season in the fall as the days begin to shorten. This seasonality ensures that lambing occurs in the spring, providing favorable weather conditions for the lambs' survival.

Ewes have an estrous cycle lasting approximately 17 days, during which they are receptive to rams for a brief period known as estrus, lasting 24 to 36 hours. Detecting when a ewe is in estrus is vital for timed mating or artificial insemination. Signs of estrus in ewes include more frequent vocalizations, restlessness, and a swollen vulva. Some farmers use marking harnesses on rams, which help identify which ewes have been bred by leaving a colored mark on the ewe's back.

For successful breeding, rams must be in good health and well-nourished, impacting their libido and sperm quality. It's advisable to conduct a breeding soundness exam on rams before the breeding season to ensure they are capable of effective breeding. This examination assesses body condition, soundness of legs and feet, and the quality and quantity of sperm.

The ratio of rams to ewes is another important consideration. Typically, one ram can service about 30 to 35 ewes during a breeding season that lasts approximately six to eight weeks. Close monitoring during this time can help manage any breeding issues that arise and ensure a high rate of pregnancy among ewes.

Pregnancy in ewes lasts around 150 days, and during this time, their nutritional needs increase, particularly in the last six weeks, when about 70% of fetal growth occurs. Proper nutrition during pregnancy is essential for the health of the ewes and the development of their lambs. Undernourishment can lead to weaker lambs at birth and higher mortality rates.

Farmers can confirm pregnancy in ewes through ultrasound, which can be performed about 45 to 60 days into the pregnancy. This method allows farmers to adjust feed rations and manage their flock based on the number of expected lambs.

Lambing is a critical time when farmers need to be vigilant and prepared to assist if complications occur. Having a lambing plan and the necessary supplies on hand, such as lambing pens, heat lamps, and colostrum or milk replacers, can make a significant difference in outcomes.

By maintaining a detailed record of breeding, pregnancy, and lambing data, farmers can analyze trends, improve their breeding strategies, and enhance overall flock productivity. Understanding and managing the breeding cycle effectively is not just about creating the next generation of sheep—it's about ensuring the sustainability and profitability of the farming operation.

Techniques for Effective Breeding

Effective breeding in sheep farming is pivotal for maintaining a healthy and productive flock. Achieving optimal reproductive success involves understanding the breeding cycle, selecting suitable breeding stock, and managing the breeding process efficiently.

Sheep typically reach sexual maturity around six to eight months of age, but it's advisable to start breeding ewes at about 18 months to ensure they've achieved sufficient body weight and are mature enough to handle pregnancy and lactation. Rams can start breeding as early as six months, but for optimal performance, many farmers wait until they are at least a year old.

Timing is critical in sheep breeding. Sheep are seasonal breeders, with most breeds cycling in the fall when daylight hours begin to decrease. This seasonality ensures that lambing occurs in the spring, maximizing lamb survival rates in favorable weather conditions. To harness this natural cycle, farmers can use light management techniques in housing to artificially extend daylight hours and stimulate out-of-season breeding if market demands or geographic conditions require it.

Choosing the right breeding stock is fundamental. This decision should be based on genetics, health, and the physical traits of both ewes and rams. It's important to maintain records of lineage to avoid inbreeding and to select traits that improve the flock's wool quality, growth rates, and overall health. Performing regular health checks and keeping up with vaccinations are crucial to ensure that both ewes and rams are in good condition for breeding.

Estrus synchronization is a technique used to have a group of ewes ovulate simultaneously. This can be beneficial for tightening the lambing period, making management easier and more efficient during lambing season. Hormonal treatments or controlled exposure to rams can trigger this synchronization.

During the mating season, farmers often employ the practice of flushing—increasing the nutrition level of ewes before and during the breeding season to enhance ovulation rates. This practice can significantly increase the number of twins and triplets born. Monitoring the body condition of ewes and adjusting their feed accordingly is vital, as both underweight and overweight animals can have reduced fertility.

Artificial insemination is another valuable technique in sheep breeding. It allows for genetic improvement by enabling the use of semen from superior rams that may be geographically distant or physically unavailable due to size or aggressiveness. It also helps control the spread of disease. However, this technique requires precise timing and skilled handling, so it may be best utilized with professional assistance.

Finally, keeping meticulous records cannot be overstated. Detailed recording of breeding dates, health status, lambing dates, and the number and condition of lambs born helps in making informed decisions about future breeding strategies and in identifying productive and less productive animals.

Caring for Ewes During Pregnancy

Caring for ewes during pregnancy is a critical component of successful sheep farming, requiring careful management and observation to ensure the health of both the ewes and their lambs. The period of gestation in ewes lasts approximately five months and can be divided into early, mid, and late stages, each with specific nutritional and medical needs.

During the early stage of pregnancy, it is crucial to maintain a stable and stress-free environment for the ewes as the risk of miscarriage is highest during the first 30 to 60 days. Farmers should avoid handling ewes roughly or changing their environment abruptly. Nutritional needs during this period do not increase significantly, but it's important to provide a balanced diet rich in vitamins and minerals to support embryo development. This includes access to high-quality forage and supplemental feed that is low in copper but rich in vitamins E, A, and D, as well as selenium to prevent White Muscle Disease in newborn lambs.

As pregnancy progresses into the mid-stage, ewes begin to require additional calories to support the developing fetuses. The quantity of feed should be increased gradually, and the diet should be adjusted to contain higher levels of energy. Good quality hay or pasture is essential, and additional protein might be necessary if forage quality is low. During this time, it's also important to monitor the body condition of the ewes and adjust feeding protocols to prevent them from becoming overweight, which can lead to birthing complications and health issues such as pregnancy toxemia.

The final stage of pregnancy is the most critical in terms of nutrition and care. Ewes' nutritional requirements peak as the lambs undergo most of their growth during this period. Farmers should provide ample amounts of high-energy feed and continue monitoring the protein intake. Overfeeding can be as detrimental as underfeeding; therefore, careful management of diet and body condition is essential. It's advisable to split feedings into smaller, more frequent meals to aid digestion and prevent bloating.

Monitoring for signs of pregnancy toxemia, especially in the last six weeks before lambing, is crucial. This condition is characterized by low blood sugar (hypoglycemia) caused by the ewes' inability to ingest enough calories to meet the metabolic demands of late pregnancy. Symptoms include lethargy, disorientation, and muscle tremors. Immediate veterinary care is required to treat this condition, often involving the administration of glucose solutions and changes in diet.

Pre-lambing preparations should include setting up a clean, dry, and well-ventilated lambing area to minimize the risk of disease and facilitate monitoring of the ewes. Farmers should also prepare lambing kits in advance, which include necessary items such as towels, iodine for treating navels, and obstetric gloves. Familiarity with the signs of labor will help farmers recognize when lambing is imminent, allowing them to provide assistance if necessary.

Regular veterinary check-ups throughout the pregnancy help monitor the health of the ewes and the development of the fetuses. Ultrasounds or manual checks can be employed to ascertain fetal numbers, which is important for feeding adjustments and lambing preparation.

Managing Lambing Season

Managing lambing season effectively is critical for the success of any sheep farm, as it directly impacts both the health of the ewes and the survival rate of the lambs. The lambing season starts with careful planning and observation, which begins months before the actual births. Farmers must ensure that their breeding practices are timed so that lambing occurs during a season that facilitates the care and survival of the newborn lambs, typically in the spring when weather conditions are milder and pasture availability is optimal.

One of the first steps in managing lambing season is to maintain the health and nutrition of the pregnant ewes. This involves providing a diet that is rich in energy, vitamins, and minerals, particularly during the last trimester when the majority of fetal growth occurs. Adequate nutrition is crucial not only for the health of the ewe but also for the proper development of the lambs. Additionally, farmers must regularly monitor the ewes for signs of distress or illness, as prompt medical intervention can prevent complications during delivery.

As the ewes approach their due dates, it's important to prepare a clean, dry, and sheltered lambing area to protect the ewes and their lambs from the elements and potential predators. The lambing area should be quiet and well-organized, with individual pens available to isolate ewes that are close to lambing. This isolation not only helps in monitoring and assisting with births but also reduces the spread of diseases.

During the actual lambing, farmers need to be vigilant and ready to assist. While many ewes can lamb without human help, complications such as dystocia (difficult labor) can arise. Knowing how to handle these situations is essential. Familiarity with basic lambing procedures, such as repositioning lambs and providing assistance when ewes are unable to deliver on their own, can significantly improve outcomes.

Immediately after birth, it is important to ensure that lambs are breathing properly and are dried off, especially in colder climates. The first few hours of life are critical, as lambs need to ingest colostrum, the nutrient-rich first milk, which is vital for building their immunity. Farmers must monitor this process closely and be prepared to hand-feed lambs if the ewe rejects them or is unable to provide sufficient milk.

After the lambs have nursed, tagging and recording their birth data is essential for managing the flock's records and future breeding decisions. This data includes the lamb's weight, the mother's identification, and any unusual circumstances or difficulties during the birth process.

Ongoing care in the weeks following birth involves regular health checks and vaccinations to protect the lambs from common diseases. Farmers also need to manage the ewes' health post-lambing, ensuring they recover fully and continue to produce enough milk for their lambs.

Finally, managing lambing season extends beyond the immediate care at birth. It involves strategic planning for weaning, integrating lambs into the flock, and possibly preparing them for sale. Each step is interconnected, and successful management depends on a comprehensive approach that considers the health and welfare of both ewes and their lambs.

CHAPTER 6

Flock Management

Herd Dynamics and Behavior Management

Understanding and managing herd dynamics and behavior is crucial in sheep farming, as it can significantly influence the health, productivity, and management ease of the flock. Sheep are social animals that naturally form groups, and their behavior within these groups can affect their stress levels, feeding patterns, breeding success, and vulnerability to predators.

The herd dynamics in sheep begin with recognizing that there are typically one or more leaders within a flock. These leaders are often older, more experienced ewes who guide the rest of the flock to grazing, water, and shelter. Observing which sheep take on these roles can help a farmer manage the flock more effectively by ensuring these leaders are healthy and well-cared for, as their behavior and health directly impact the rest of the flock.

Social hierarchy within a flock also affects feeding behavior. Sheep establish a pecking order, and those lower in the hierarchy may be pushed away from feed or choice grazing areas by more dominant individuals. This can lead to uneven nutrition and growth rates within the flock. To manage this, farmers can implement feeding strategies that ensure all sheep have equal access to food, such as multiple feeding stations or larger feeding areas that prevent crowding.

Breeding behavior is another aspect influenced by herd dynamics. Dominant males may monopolize breeding opportunities, which can skew genetic diversity if not managed properly. Farmers can manage breeding through controlled mating practices, ensuring that a broader genetic mix is maintained by rotating rams in and out of the flock or using artificial insemination techniques with sperm from genetically diverse rams.

Stress management is crucial, as high stress levels can lead to health problems and reduced productivity. Stress in sheep can be caused by factors such as improper handling, inadequate space, and poor social interactions. Implementing gentle handling techniques, providing adequate space, and maintaining stable groupings without frequent changes can help reduce stress. Sheep are creatures of habit, and maintaining a consistent routine helps keep the flock calm and cooperative.

Predator management is also linked to herd behavior. Sheep naturally group together for protection against predators. Enhancing this natural behavior by providing secure fencing, guard animals like dogs, llamas, or donkeys, and maintaining visibility in grazing areas can help protect the flock from predators. Additionally, ensuring that the flock's leaders are vigilant and healthy can enhance the natural vigilance of the group.

Lastly, understanding and managing lambing behavior within the flock is important for lamb survival and ewe health. Ewes often seek isolation for lambing, which can be challenging in a tightly managed space. Providing areas where ewes can have some privacy during lambing season can lead to better outcomes in terms of lamb mortality and ewe health.

Training and Handling Techniques

Training and handling sheep effectively is crucial for both the safety of the animals and the ease of managing a flock. Good training techniques start from the early days of a lamb's life. Handling lambs frequently and gently helps them grow accustomed to human contact, which facilitates future interactions such as health checks and shearing.

One effective approach to training sheep involves using positive reinforcement. Sheep respond well to rewards, which can be in the form of food treats or even simple verbal praise and gentle petting when they follow commands or allow themselves to be handled without resistance. Establishing a routine is also beneficial. Regular feeding times, shearing, and health checks can help condition the sheep to expect and accept these activities without stress.

Sheep are naturally gregarious animals that follow a leader. This trait can be leveraged in training by identifying and training a lead sheep in the flock to follow commands, with the expectation that the others will follow. Using a lead sheep simplifies processes like moving the flock from one pasture to another or leading them into handling facilities.

Handling techniques must prioritize safety and minimize stress. Sheep should never be lifted by their wool as this can cause pain and potentially injure their skin or muscles. Instead, handlers should use the base of the horn and the area around the neck or hindquarters when needing to direct or stabilize a sheep physically.

Creating a low-stress environment is essential during any handling process. Facilities used for shearing, health examinations, or transport should be designed to allow smooth movement of sheep and reduce opportunities for injuries. Features such as non-slip surfaces, adequate space, and absence of sharp corners are important.

Additionally, it is crucial to train and familiarize sheep with different handling facilities and procedures gradually. Acclimatizing sheep to these environments during non-stressful times can significantly reduce their anxiety during actual handling processes. For instance, allowing sheep to explore a trailer calmly and at their own pace before they are ever loaded for transport can make the actual experience much less stressful.

Regular handling not only makes sheep easier to manage but also allows for better monitoring of their health and well-being. Familiarity with human contact means sheep are less likely to hide symptoms of illness or injury, allowing for quicker interventions.

Tools and Equipment Needed for Effective Flock Management

Effective flock management requires a variety of tools and equipment that are essential for maintaining the health, productivity, and well-being of sheep. One of the primary tools in sheep farming is a good quality fencing system. Fences need to be secure enough to keep sheep within designated grazing areas while protecting them from predators. Electric fencing is particularly effective for its portability, which facilitates rotational grazing—a practice that prevents pasture overgrazing and reduces the risk of parasite infestation.

Shepherds also rely heavily on shearing equipment. Electric shears are preferred for their efficiency, especially for larger flocks. These shears require regular maintenance, including sharpening and lubrication, to ensure they function effectively and safely. Alongside shears, hoof trimmers are vital for routine sheep care. Regular hoof trimming prevents foot rot and other hoof-related diseases that can severely affect a sheep's mobility and overall health.

For handling and moving sheep, crooks and hurdles are indispensable. A shepherd's crook, typically with a hook at one end, is used to catch individual sheep around the neck or leg, facilitating examination and treatment. Hurdles are portable fence panels used to create temporary pens or to guide sheep in a desired direction, particularly useful during feeding or when administering medical treatment.

Watering systems are essential to provide clean and continuous water supply, especially in large pastures. Automatic waterers save labor and ensure that sheep have access to fresh water at all times, reducing the risk of dehydration and heat stress.

To monitor the health and productivity of the flock, a variety of health management tools are needed. This includes scales for weighing sheep to monitor their growth and condition, which can indicate health issues early. Tagging equipment for ear tags helps in the identification and tracking of individual animals for breeding, health management, and sales records.

Additionally, a well-equipped first aid kit is crucial for dealing with injuries or illnesses until veterinary care can be accessed. This should include antiseptics, bandages, wound ointments, antibiotics, and tools for administering medications, such as syringes and drench guns.

Lastly, record-keeping tools are vital. Maintaining accurate records of breeding, health, sales, and financial transactions is necessary for successful flock management. Software specifically designed for agricultural management can greatly enhance the efficiency of record-keeping, allowing for easy tracking of individual sheep histories and flock trends over time.

CHAPTER 7

Wool and Shearing

Best Practices for Wool Production

Wool production is a vital aspect of raising sheep and can be quite lucrative with the right practices. To achieve high-quality wool, the breed of sheep is crucial. Breeds such as Merino, Corriedale, and Rambouillet are known for their superior fleece quality. It is essential for farmers to select the right breed based on the climate and the wool characteristics they aim to produce.

The care and health of the sheep play a significant role in the quality of the wool. Sheep should be fed a balanced diet rich in nutrients that promote healthy fleece. This includes a mix of grasses, supplemented with grains and minerals, especially during the colder months when pasture quality decreases. Regular access to clean water is also essential as it impacts the sheep's overall health and the quality of their wool.

Parasite control is another critical factor in wool production. Parasites can damage the skin and fleece, leading to poor wool quality and even wool loss. Regular deworming and flock inspections help maintain the health of the sheep and the integrity of the wool.

Shearing is best done in the early spring before the sheep lamb and the weather becomes too hot. Shearing before lambing not only reduces stress on the sheep but also results in cleaner wool since sheep tend to get dirtier during lambing. Shearing should be performed carefully to avoid cutting the skin of the sheep, which can cause infections and damage the fleece.

The tools used for shearing need to be well-maintained and sharp. Dull blades can pull at the wool, causing discomfort to the sheep and potentially damaging the fleece. Proper shearing technique is important; the shearer should be trained to efficiently remove the fleece in one piece, which protects the animal and results in a higher quality product.

After shearing, the wool must be properly handled to maintain its quality. It should be skirted to remove any dirty or inferior parts and then graded according to fiber diameter, length, and color. Proper storage of the wool is crucial to prevent damage from moisture and pests. The wool should be kept in a clean, dry environment until it can be processed.

Processing the wool involves cleaning it thoroughly to remove dirt, grease, and other contaminants. This is typically done through a series of washes and rinses. Once cleaned, the wool can be carded, which helps to align the fibers and prepare them for spinning. The final quality of the wool fabric also depends on the spinning, knitting, or weaving processes used.

Marketing wool products effectively requires knowledge of the market and customer preferences. Offering detailed information about the wool's characteristics and the sustainable practices used in its production can attract customers looking for high-quality, eco-friendly products.

Shearing Techniques and Tools

Shearing sheep is an essential aspect of managing a flock, primarily for wool production and the health of the animals. Traditionally, shearing occurs once or twice a year, depending on the breed and climate, to prevent the sheep from overheating in summer and to reduce the risk of parasitic infestations and skin diseases.

The most common technique for shearing sheep is the electric shears method, which is efficient and quick. Before beginning the shearing process, it is crucial to ensure that the sheep are dry, as wet wool can clog shears and make the process difficult and uncomfortable for both the animal and the shearer. Shearers usually start by shearing the belly and removing the dirty wool around the tail and hind legs, which is typically not used for high-quality wool products.

After the belly, shearers move to the back and sides of the sheep, carefully removing the fleece in smooth, even strokes to maintain the quality of the wool and avoid second cuts or nicks in the skin. The quality of the fleece is preserved by keeping the shears flat against the body and working in a pattern that allows the wool to come off in one piece.

The headpiece and electric shears are the most widely used tools. A good pair of shears will have different speed settings and sharp, durable blades that can be easily replaced. It is essential for shearers to maintain their equipment, as dull blades can pull the wool instead of cutting it, causing discomfort to the sheep.

For those new to shearing, pneumatic shears might be another option to consider. They are easier on the hands and arms, reducing fatigue and the risk of repetitive strain injuries, which are common among professional shearers. However, they require access to an air compressor, which can be a limitation in more remote areas.

Hand shears, although not commonly used for commercial shearing, still play a significant role in small flocks or for shepherds who prefer a more traditional approach. Hand shearing requires more skill and strength but offers greater control over the cut, which can be beneficial for avoiding cuts to the skin in particularly sensitive areas or with particularly wriggly sheep.

Sheep should be handled gently and calmly during shearing to minimize stress. The use of a shearing table or stand can help at reducing the physical strain on the shearer and keeping the sheep secure during the process. Proper technique involves the shearer holding the sheep between their legs, controlling the movement with their knees and feet. This allows for quick and safe shearing, keeping both the shearer and the sheep as comfortable as possible.

After shearing, it's important to manage the wool correctly. Wool should be skirted to remove any dirty or low-quality parts and then graded and baled according to quality standards. Proper wool management ensures maximum profitability from the fleece and contributes to a sustainable farming practice.

In addition to shearing, regular hoof trimming and health checks should be integrated into the shearing routine, making it an opportunity to assess each animal for other health issues such as lumps, cuts, or infections that might need attention.

Processing and Selling Wool

Processing and selling wool is a vital aspect of sheep farming for many producers, turning a necessary maintenance activity into a potentially lucrative aspect of the business. Once sheep are shorn, the raw wool must be properly handled to maximize its quality and market value. The first step in wool processing is skirting, which involves removing the dirtiest and coarsest parts of the fleece, typically found around the edges. This step is crucial as it significantly influences the cleanliness and overall quality of the wool, which are key factors in determining its market price.

After skirting, the wool is graded and sorted based on fiber diameter, length, crimp, and color. These characteristics determine the wool's end use, whether for fine clothing, coarser fabrics, or other wool products. Sorting and grading require a good understanding of wool characteristics and market demands. Farmers can either learn to perform these tasks themselves or hire experienced wool classers to ensure their wool fetches the best market prices.

The next phase involves washing the wool to remove grease (lanolin), dirt, and other contaminants. This is typically done using a series of warm water baths with detergents that are gentle on the fibers but effective in cleaning. Care must be taken to prevent felting, which can occur if the wool fibers are agitated too much during the washing process.

Once cleaned, the wool is dried, often in well-ventilated areas to ensure even drying without exposure to direct sunlight, which can degrade the fibers. After drying, the wool is carded, a process that aligns the fibers and prepares them for spinning. Carding can be done with hand-operated tools for small-scale producers or with large carding machines for larger volumes.

Spinning transforms the carded wool into yarn by twisting the fibers together. The thickness of the yarn and the tightness of the twist depend on the intended use of the wool product. After spinning, the yarn can be dyed, a step that should be handled carefully to maintain fiber integrity while achieving vibrant, long-lasting colors.

Once processed, the wool is ready for sale, either as raw fiber, spun yarn, or even as finished goods like blankets, clothing, or other crafts. Marketing wool effectively requires understanding the target market, whether local craft markets, online platforms, or larger distributors specializing in textile supplies. Pricing should reflect the quality of the wool, the labor involved in processing, and the current market conditions.

Farmers can increase their wool's marketability by maintaining high standards of animal welfare and ensuring that their sheep produce high-quality fleece. Some markets are particularly interested in wool from sheep that have been raised in specific, humane conditions, such as free-range environments, and this can be used as a marketing point. Furthermore, establishing a brand that tells a story, emphasizing aspects such as sustainability and local production, can also attract customers willing to pay a premium for ethically produced, high-quality wool.

Finally, building relationships with buyers, attending wool and agricultural shows, and engaging in wool industry associations can provide valuable networking opportunities and insights into trends and innovations in wool processing and sales. By understanding the complete process from shearing to sale, sheep farmers can add significant value to their operations and ensure a profitable and sustainable business.

CHAPTER 8

Marketing Your Products

Understanding the Market for Sheep Products

When venturing into the sheep farming business, understanding the market dynamics for sheep products is crucial for profitability. Sheep products encompass a variety of items, including wool, meat (lamb and mutton), milk, and even pelts. Each of these products has its own market with specific demands and trends that a farmer must grasp to optimize sales and revenue.

Wool is one of the primary products derived from sheep. The demand for wool varies greatly depending on its quality, which is influenced by the breed of sheep, their diet, and the shearing methods used. Fine wool is highly prized in the fashion industry for making garments, while coarser wool is often used in carpets and upholstery. Keeping abreast of fashion trends and textile industry needs can help farmers target their wool production to meet market demands more effectively.

Lamb and mutton are the meat products obtained from sheep. Lamb, being the meat from younger sheep, is generally more tender and fetches a higher price in the market. Mutton, from older sheep, is richer in flavor but less tender, appealing to a different consumer base. Ethnic and religious demographics play significant roles in the consumption patterns of lamb and mutton. For instance, lamb is particularly popular during certain religious festivities in various cultures, which can lead to seasonal spikes in demand. Farmers can benefit from these insights by timing their production cycles to coincide with these peak periods.

Sheep's milk is another valuable product, though less common in the U.S. market compared to Europe and parts of Asia. It is rich in fats and proteins and is often used to make specialty cheeses like Roquefort, pecorino, and feta. These cheeses are typically higher priced and can offer significant profit margins if produced and marketed effectively. Understanding the niche markets for sheep's milk and its byproducts can open up lucrative avenues for farmers willing to invest in dairy sheep breeds.

In addition to these primary products, sheep pelts are used in fashion and home decoration. The quality of pelts, like wool, depends on the breed and care of the sheep. Markets for pelts can be variable and influenced by fashion trends, requiring farmers to stay informed about the industry's current preferences.

Farmers must also consider their local and national markets. While local markets allow for direct sales and potentially higher margins through farm-to-table setups, national markets can offer larger volume sales but may require more effort in logistics and adherence to stricter regulations.

Marketing strategies for sheep products include both traditional and digital approaches. Farmers markets, direct sales to restaurants, and participation in agricultural fairs remain effective for reaching local consumers. For broader reach, developing a strong online presence through a farm website, social media marketing, and partnerships with online retailers can significantly increase sales channels.

Lastly, sustainable and ethical farming practices have become increasingly important to consumers. Certifications such as organic, grass-fed, or animal welfare-approved can enhance product value and appeal to a broader audience, often allowing farmers to command higher prices.

Strategies for Marketing Meat, Wool, and Live Animals

Marketing meat, wool, and live animals effectively requires a well-rounded strategy that considers both traditional and digital platforms to reach potential buyers. For sheep farmers, understanding the market dynamics and buyer preferences is crucial. Sheep products can cater to various markets, from local butchers and restaurants looking for quality meat, to textile manufacturers in need of raw wool, and even fellow farmers or breeders interested in purchasing live animals.

Starting with meat, the primary concern is quality and compliance with local regulations regarding health and safety. Farmers should build relationships with local butchers and gourmet restaurants that prioritize farm-to-table supply chains. Participating in farmer's markets or creating a subscription service for regular meat deliveries can also help in establishing a direct connection with consumers who value fresh, organically raised meat. Additionally, offering unique products such as lamb sausages or smoked cuts can distinguish a farm's offerings from competitors.

Wool presents a fantastic opportunity due to its renewable nature and wide range of uses, from clothing to insulation materials. To market wool effectively, farmers should focus on the fiber's quality and the ethical aspects of their farming practices, which are highly valued in markets sensitive to animal welfare and environmental impact. Establishing connections with local artisans, craft shops, and larger textile processors can open various channels for wool sales. Online platforms like Etsy or eBay can also be utilized to reach broader markets. Participating in wool shows or fiber festivals can further expand visibility and networking opportunities.

When it comes to selling live animals, the focus shifts to the genetic quality, health, and breed characteristics of the sheep. Sales can be maximized through breeding high-demand breeds known for their meat, wool quality, or hardiness in various climates. Maintaining meticulous health records and breeding histories increases the value of live animals and builds trust with potential buyers. Farmers can market live animals through agricultural shows, online livestock marketplaces, or through direct partnerships with other farms.

Digital marketing plays a crucial role in modern agricultural sales strategies. Creating a robust online presence through a farm website, active social media profiles, and email marketing campaigns can help farmers reach a wider audience. Educational content about the benefits of sheep products, along with regular updates from the farm, can engage potential customers and create a loyal consumer base.

Lastly, all marketing efforts should be backed by good customer relationships. Whether through excellent customer service, transparency about farming practices, or simply sharing the stories behind the farm and its sheep, building a strong rapport with customers can lead to repeat business and referrals which are invaluable for sustained success in the competitive market of sheep products.

Online and Offline Marketing Techniques

Marketing products from sheep farming, such as wool, meat, and live animals, requires a strategic blend of both online and offline techniques to maximize reach and profitability.

Starting with online marketing, establishing a strong digital presence is crucial. Creating a website can serve as the central hub for your business where customers can learn about your farm, the products you offer, and how they are produced. This site should include high-quality images of your flock and products, detailed descriptions, and perhaps a blog to share updates, farming tips, or features on specific animals. Social media platforms like Facebook, Instagram, and Twitter are excellent tools for building community engagement. They allow farmers to post updates, run promotions, and interact with consumers and other farmers. Additionally, email newsletters can be used to keep your audience informed about new stock, upcoming events, or special deals.

E-commerce is another vital component of the online strategy. Selling products directly from your website or through online marketplaces can significantly expand your customer base beyond local boundaries. This approach is particularly effective for products like wool, which can be shipped easily. Consider using online ads to reach a broader audience. Platforms such as Google Ads or Facebook Ads can target specific demographics who are most likely to be interested in your products.

Turning to offline marketing, attending local farmers' markets and agricultural shows is a highly effective way to meet customers face-to-face and sell your products directly. These events provide the opportunity for potential buyers to see and touch your wool, taste your meat products, and even meet the animals, creating a direct connection to your farm. Networking at these events can also lead to partnerships with other local businesses or larger contracts for meat and wool supply.

Additionally, traditional advertising methods such as local newspaper ads, radio spots, and flyers can be used to raise awareness about your farm within the community. Offering farm tours and hosting open days can attract local visitors, who might then share their experiences via word of mouth, one of the most powerful marketing tools available.

For those selling meat, developing relationships with local restaurants and butchers can establish a steady demand for your products. Providing them with high-quality, locally raised meat can lead to long-term business relationships. It's also beneficial to get your products certified as organic or grass-fed if applicable, as this can be a significant selling point.

Another effective offline strategy is to engage in community outreach by participating in local events, sponsoring community projects, or holding educational workshops on sheep farming. These activities not only market your products but also build your farm's reputation as a community-minded business.

CHAPTER 9

Pasture and Land Management

Basics of Pasture Layout and Design

When designing a pasture for sheep, the goal is to create a sustainable environment that meets the nutritional needs of the sheep while managing the land effectively. A well-planned pasture layout supports healthy growth in sheep, prevents overgrazing, and minimizes the need for supplemental feeding.

The first step in pasture design is understanding the land available. Assessing the soil type, topography, and native vegetation is crucial. Different soil types can affect water drainage and the types of grasses or legumes that can be planted. Ideally, pasture land should have a mix of flat areas and gentle slopes to promote exercise and natural grazing behaviors while ensuring good drainage.

The size of the pasture should accommodate the number of sheep, allowing for adequate grazing space. A common rule of thumb is to provide at least one to two acres per five sheep, but this can vary based on soil fertility, grass type, and climate. Rotational grazing is a beneficial practice, where sheep are moved between multiple pastures to allow grass to recover and regrow. This method not only maintains a healthy pasture but also reduces the parasite load in the environment, as parasites don't have time to complete their lifecycle before sheep are moved to a new area.

Fencing is critical in pasture design, both to keep sheep safely contained and to protect them from predators. Fences should be sturdy and tall enough to prevent sheep from jumping over. Mesh wire fencing is often used because it prevents lambs from escaping and deters predators.

Water access is another essential component. Sheep need a consistent supply of clean water, and water sources should be easy to access and maintain. Placing water troughs strategically in all pastures ensures that sheep can hydrate without having to travel too far, which is especially important during hot weather.

The types of grasses planted in a pasture also play a significant role in the overall health of the flock. Grasses like ryegrass, bluegrass, and fescue are popular because of their resilience and nutritional value. Including legumes such as clover or alfalfa can enhance the nutritional content of the pasture, reducing the need for supplemental feeds. These plants also help in fixing nitrogen in the soil, improving soil fertility.

Managing weeds and pests is vital for maintaining a healthy pasture. Regular mowing, controlled burns, or grazing management can prevent weeds from taking over. It's also essential to work with an agronomist or a local extension service to identify and treat any pest issues specific to the area.

Rotational Grazing Systems

Rotational grazing is a method where sheep are moved between different pastures or sections of a pasture to prevent overgrazing and to allow grass to regenerate. This system not only enhances pasture productivity but also improves the overall health of the flock. It involves dividing a larger pasture into smaller, manageable sections, often called paddocks, and systematically rotating the sheep through these sections in a planned sequence.

The primary advantage of rotational grazing is the maintenance and improvement of pasture quality. By allowing grasses time to recover after grazing, they can regrow to a more beneficial stage for both the plant's life cycle and the dietary needs of sheep. This regrowth period is critical because it helps to develop a robust root system, which in turn stabilizes the soil and improves its fertility through natural processes such as nitrogen fixation in some plant species.

Another significant benefit of rotational grazing is the reduction of parasites, which are common in sheep and can severely affect their health and productivity. Parasites tend to thrive in conditions where sheep graze close to the ground. Rotating pastures allows grasses to grow taller, which reduces the sheep's exposure to these parasites, as they are less likely to graze near parasite-infected areas. Additionally, the lifecycle of parasites is disrupted by the absence of hosts in recently grazed paddocks, thereby decreasing the overall parasite load.

Implementing a rotational grazing system requires initial planning and investment. Farmers must first assess their land to determine the carrying capacity, which is the number of animals the land can support without causing environmental degradation. Based on this assessment, the land is then divided into paddocks that are sized to sustain the flock for a short period, typically 3-7 days, although this can vary based on specific conditions like soil fertility, pasture species, and weather patterns.

Water access is a crucial factor in rotational grazing. Each paddock should have a reliable water source for the sheep, as moving water systems can be costly and labor-intensive. Portable water tanks or a series of troughs connected to a central water system can efficiently provide water across various paddocks.

Fencing is another essential component. Temporary electric fencing is popular for rotational grazing as it is relatively inexpensive, flexible, and easy to move. Permanent fencing can also be used for outer boundaries, with temporary fences subdividing the internal areas.

Rotational grazing is not just beneficial for the land and sheep but also for the environment. By enhancing ground cover and reducing soil erosion, it helps in carbon sequestration, which is the process of capturing and storing atmospheric carbon dioxide. It also promotes biodiversity by allowing various plants and wildlife to thrive in different sections of the pasture at different times.

Land Maintenance and Sustainability Practices

Maintaining land and implementing sustainability practices are critical components of successful sheep farming. Healthy pastures not only provide the primary food source for sheep but also play a vital role in the ecological balance, helping to prevent soil erosion, improve soil fertility, and support biodiversity.

Effective pasture management starts with understanding the type of grasses and plants that are best suited to the local climate and soil conditions. Sheep farmers often prefer a mix of grasses because they provide a balanced diet for the flock and are resilient to grazing pressure. Rotational grazing is a key technique where sheep are moved between different pasture sections to prevent overgrazing. This method allows grasses to recover and grow back healthier, which in turn supports the sheep with optimal nutrition.

Soil health is another cornerstone of sustainable land management. Regular testing of soil can inform the farmer about nutrient deficiencies, which can be addressed through natural fertilizers like composted manure from the sheep themselves. This not only recycles waste but also reduces the reliance on chemical fertilizers, which can be harmful to the environment.

Water management also plays a crucial role. Ensuring that pastures have adequate drainage prevents erosion and waterlogging, which can lead to plant death and reduced grazing area. Conversely, during dry periods, having an efficient water system can keep pastures green and lush without wasteful overuse of water.

To further enhance sustainability, farmers can plant trees around pastures to provide shade for sheep, reduce wind speed at ground level, and improve the capture of atmospheric carbon. Trees and shrubs can also act as natural windbreaks and contribute to the biodiversity of the farm by providing habitats for wildlife.

Managing weeds in pastures requires careful consideration. Instead of relying on herbicides, more sustainable practices include using rotational grazing to reduce weed growth and introducing specific plant species that naturally outcompete common weeds. In some cases, biological control methods, such as introducing insects that feed on certain weeds, can also be effective.

Another aspect of sustainability in sheep farming is managing the flock's size according to the land's carrying capacity. Overstocking can lead to overgrazing, soil compaction, and a significant drop in pasture quality. By keeping the flock size within the limits of what the land can sustain, farmers ensure that their practices can be maintained year after year without degrading resources.

Finally, farmers are increasingly adopting modern technologies like GPS and drone surveillance to monitor pasture conditions and herd movements, enabling more precise and less intrusive land management.

CHAPTER 10

Legal and Financial Management

Understanding Local Regulations and Permits

Navigating the maze of local regulations and permits is crucial for anyone planning to raise sheep, as compliance ensures both the legality and smooth operation of your farming venture. Each state and even local municipalities may have their own specific requirements, and understanding these is key to avoiding legal complications that could disrupt your farm.

In the United States, sheep farmers must first ensure they meet zoning requirements. Agricultural zoning laws dictate where livestock farms can operate, and some residential areas might restrict the practice. Before purchasing land or starting your sheep farm, check with your local zoning board to ensure that your land is zoned for livestock. If it's not, you may need to apply for a variance or reconsider your location.

Another critical area of regulation is environmental protection. Livestock farms are subject to regulations designed to protect the environment from pollution. This includes managing manure to prevent contamination of water supplies, soil, and air quality. Farmers need to develop a manure management plan that complies with state regulations, which might involve installing waste storage facilities, utilizing proper disposal techniques, and regular testing of water sources.

Animal welfare laws also play a significant role in sheep farming. These regulations ensure the humane treatment of animals and cover aspects such as feeding, housing, and general care. Compliance with these laws not only protects the animals but also supports the farm's public image and marketability. It's important to stay updated on these regulations, as they can change and vary widely between regions.

Disease control measures are equally important. Many states require health certificates and veterinary inspections for livestock. These measures help prevent the spread of diseases such as scrapie, a degenerative disease affecting the central nervous system of sheep. Participation in voluntary disease control programs like the Scrapie Eradication Program can also be beneficial, providing access to tags and tracking systems that help manage and eradicate the disease.

When it comes to selling sheep or sheep products, additional regulations may apply. These include health and safety standards for meat processing and labeling requirements for meat and wool products. Selling meat, in particular, requires compliance with federal and state health regulations, which might involve inspections by the USDA or state agencies.

Lastly, obtaining the necessary permits and maintaining good records are vital for legal compliance and financial management. Proper documentation of purchases, health records, breeding records, and sales can not only help in regulatory compliance but also assist in tax preparation and financial analysis.

Financial Planning and Record Keeping

Financial planning and record keeping are crucial components of managing a successful sheep farm. Effective financial management begins with a clear understanding of both initial investment and ongoing operational costs. For a sheep farm, initial costs typically include the purchase of land, sheep, fencing, and basic infrastructure like barns and water systems. Additionally, starting capital must cover initial feed and veterinary expenses until the farm becomes self-sustaining.

Operational expenses for sheep farming include the cost of feed, healthcare, shearing supplies, and labor. It's also important to plan for unexpected costs such as veterinary emergencies or price fluctuations in feed. To manage these costs, sheep farmers should set up a detailed budget that outlines expected monthly and annual expenses and income. This budget should be reviewed and adjusted annually to reflect changes in market conditions, production levels, and farm goals.

Income for sheep farms can come from several sources including the sale of wool, meat, and breeding stock. Diversifying income sources can provide financial stability. For example, selling wool and meat in local markets or directly to consumers often fetches a better price than wholesale channels. Additionally, offering agritourism activities like farm tours or shearing demonstrations can provide additional revenue streams.

Record keeping is another essential aspect of sheep farming, serving both practical farm management and legal compliance purposes. Maintaining accurate health records helps in monitoring the well-being of the flock and scheduling routine veterinary care, which is essential for maintaining the health of the sheep and the profitability of the farm. These records should include details of vaccinations, deworming, and any other treatments or medical incidents.

Financial records are equally important. They should meticulously track all income and expenses. This not only helps in financial planning and budgeting but is also critical for tax purposes. Good record keeping makes it easier to fill out tax returns accurately and can help in claiming deductions on farm expenses which can significantly lower tax liabilities.

Moreover, if the farm is subject to inspections or audits, having detailed and organized records can demonstrate compliance with local and federal agricultural regulations. This includes records of animal sales and purchases which often need to be reported to agricultural agencies.

Lastly, long-term financial planning should include strategies for reinvestment in the farm and retirement planning for the farmer. Reinvestment might involve upgrading infrastructure, purchasing additional sheep, or investing in more efficient technology to improve farm productivity. Planning for the future ensures that the farm remains viable and competitive in the long term, securing a sustainable operation that can support the farmer and potentially future generations.

Risk Management and Insurance for Sheep Farms

Risk management and insurance are crucial components of running a successful sheep farm. Sheep farming, like any agricultural venture, comes with its own set of risks. These include natural disasters, disease outbreaks, predation, and market fluctuations, all of which can significantly impact the financial stability and operational continuity of a farm.

One of the first steps in managing risks is to conduct a thorough assessment of the potential hazards that could affect the farm. Farmers should consider the local climate and environmental conditions that might predispose their operations to certain risks, such as floods, drought, or wildfires. Additionally, understanding the prevalence of diseases and the types of predators in the region can help in planning adequate preventive measures.

After identifying the risks, implementing preventive measures is the next critical step. This could involve constructing sturdy, weather-resistant shelters to protect the sheep from harsh conditions, or setting up fencing and security systems to prevent attacks from predators. Regular health checks and adherence to vaccination schedules can mitigate the risk of disease outbreaks, which are not only costly but can also lead to broader biosecurity concerns.

Despite the best preventive measures, not all risks can be entirely eliminated. This is where insurance comes into play. Sheep farmers should explore various insurance options that provide coverage for different aspects of their operation. Livestock insurance can cover losses due to death from disease or accidents, while crop insurance might be necessary if the farm grows its own feed. Property insurance is essential to protect buildings and equipment from damage or loss due to events like fires or storms.

Comprehensive general liability insurance is also important as it protects the farm from legal claims in case of accidents that may occur on the property, involving employees or visitors. For farms that engage in direct sales or agritourism activities, this type of insurance becomes even more critical.

Another aspect of risk management is financial planning. Sheep farmers should maintain a reserve fund to handle unexpected expenses that may not be covered by insurance. This financial buffer can help ensure the farm remains operational while recovering from a significant loss or during periods of market downturns.

Market risks can be managed by diversifying income streams. Instead of relying solely on one product such as wool, meat, or breeding stock, farmers can explore a combination of these. Value-added products, such as artisan cheeses or yarn, can also provide additional revenue sources that might be more resistant to market fluctuations.

Finally, staying informed about changes in agricultural regulations and market conditions is vital. Compliance with local, state, and federal regulations not only prevents legal complications but can also open up opportunities for government assistance programs, which may offer financial aid in the event of disaster or economic hardship.

By adopting a comprehensive approach to risk management and insurance, sheep farmers can protect their investments and ensure the long-term sustainability of their farms.

CHAPTER 11

Conclusion

Successfully raising sheep requires a combination of knowledge, dedication, and a proactive approach to managing the myriad challenges that come with animal husbandry. Sheep farming can be immensely rewarding, providing not only a source of income but also a way of life that connects farmers with the land and the natural cycle of life. The keys to success involve understanding the specific needs and behaviors of sheep, maintaining their health through proper nutrition and disease prevention, and managing breeding and flock dynamics effectively.

One of the most critical aspects is learning from experience. Each day on a sheep farm brings new lessons as each season cycles through. Successful sheep farmers are those who adapt to changing conditions, whether they are shifts in the market, environmental challenges, or advancements in agricultural practices. Engaging with local farming communities and continuing education through workshops and agricultural extension programs can also significantly enhance a farmer's knowledge and adaptability.

Additionally, embracing sustainability not only ensures the health of the flock but also the long-term viability of the farm's surrounding environment. Practices such as rotational grazing help maintain the health of pastures, reducing erosion and improving soil quality, which in turn supports healthier crops and animals.

Marketing is another crucial component. Understanding the market dynamics for wool, meat, and even dairy products from sheep can help farmers make informed decisions about managing their operations. The development of a strong business plan that includes diversified income streams and a marketing strategy can help stabilize income, making the farming enterprise more resilient to fluctuations in any one area of the market.

Finally, it's important for those entering sheep farming to do so with realistic expectations. While it offers a unique and fulfilling way of life, it also demands hard work, persistence, and a willingness to face the challenges head-on. With the right preparation and resources, such as comprehensive guides like "How to Raise Sheep," new farmers can equip themselves with the tools needed to build thriving, sustainable sheep farms. Such endeavors not only support individual families and businesses but also contribute to the broader agricultural community, ensuring the preservation and growth of this important sector.

Printed in Great Britain
by Amazon